THE
BIG
TIME

ROBERT GRIFFIN III

VALERIE BODDEN

CREATIVE EDUCATION

ROBERT GRIFFIN III

TABLE OF CONTENTS

MEET ROBERT

Robert gets the football. A big defender runs toward him as he throws a pass down the field to a teammate. Robert is hit hard and knocked down. But he sees his teammate make the catch for a touchdown!

obert Griffin III is a star quarterback for the Washington Redskins. He has a strong arm and fast legs. He is a smart leader, too. Robert's fans call him RG3. He is one of the most exciting players in the National Football League (NFL).

Robert's team plays at FedExField

ROBERT'S CHILDHOOD

Robert was born February 12, 1990, in Japan. His parents were serving in the United States Army there. Robert had two older sisters. The family moved to Copperas Cove, Texas, before Robert started school.

Robert and his family were happy he joined the NFL

COPPERAS COVE, TEXAS

GETTING INTO FOOTBALL

Robert learned to play basketball and baseball in elementary school. In high school, he played football and basketball and ran *track*. Robert got good grades. He graduated from high school five months early.

Robert worked out along a Texas road when he was in high school

In January 2008, Robert started college at Baylor University. He studied **political science** and played quarterback on the football team. In 2011, Robert led the Baylor Bears to 10 wins and just 3 losses. He won the Heisman Trophy as college football's best player.

Robert was known as a fast-running quarterback in college

THE BIG TIME

In January 2012, Robert decided he would go into the NFL. He was ***drafted*** by the Washington Redskins. He was the second player picked in the NFL Draft that year.

Redskins fans were excited about Robert playing for their team

In Robert's first NFL game, he threw for more than 300 yards! He also *rushed* for more than 40 yards to help the Redskins win the game. Robert was named *Rookie* of the Month for September 2012.

··

After the 2012 season, Robert won the Offensive Rookie of the Year award

OFF THE FIELD

When he is not playing football, Robert likes to spend time with his family and his *fiancée*. He likes to stay at home to watch movies or play video games. Fans noticed that Robert always wore fun socks, too.

Robert showing off his monster socks (left) and with fiancée Rebecca (right)

WHAT IS NEXT?

In Robert's first season, the Redskins lost six out of the first nine games. But Robert worked hard to make himself and his team better, and they finished with 10 wins in 2012. He hoped to someday lead his team to the Super Bowl!

....

Robert (#10) and his teammates took first place in their division in 2012

WHAT ROBERT SAYS ABOUT ...

HIS PARENTS

"My parents were huge on discipline.... And if you say you're going to start something, you finish it."

LOSING

"I don't like losing. You just try to make sure guys know that this stuff is serious, it means something to me personally, and it should mean something to them as well."

THE NFL

"Just playing in the NFL is an honor. It's a lot of fun. People don't realize that."

GLOSSARY

drafted picked to be on a team; in a sports draft, teams take turns choosing players

fiancée a woman who has promised to marry someone

political science the study of how governments work

rookie a player in his first season

rushed ran with the football

track a sport that includes races on a round track

READ MORE

Frisch, Aaron. *Washington Redskins.* Mankato, Minn.: Creative Education, 2011.

MacRae, Sloan. *The Washington Redskins.* New York: PowerKids Press, 2011.

WEBSITES

Pro Football Reference
http://www.pro-football-reference.com/ players/G/GrifRo01.htm
This page lists Robert's statistics and all the honors he has won.

Washington Redskins Kids Club
http://www.redskinskidsclub.com/
This is the kids' website for Robert's team, the Washington Redskins.

INDEX

PUBLISHED BY Creative Education
P.O. Box 227, Mankato, Minnesota 56002
Creative Education is an imprint of The Creative Company
www.thecreativecompany.us

DESIGN AND PRODUCTION BY Christine Vanderbeek
ART DIRECTION BY Rita Marshall
PRINTED IN the United States of America

PHOTOGRAPHS BY Corbis (Cliff Welch/Icon SMI), Getty Images (Al Bello, Rob Carr, Max Faulkner/Fort Worth Star-Telegram/MCT, Ronald Martinez, Jamie McCarthy, Patrick McDermott, John McDonnell/The Washington Post, Jonathan Newton/The Washington Post, Joe Robbins, Rob Tringali/SportsChrome), iStockphoto (Anthia Cumming, Pingebat), Shutterstock (Helga Esteb)

LIBRARY OF CONGRESS CATALOGING-IN-PUBLICATION DATA
Bodden, Valerie.
Robert Griffin III / Valerie Bodden.
p. cm. — (The big time)
Includes index.
Summary: An elementary introduction to the life, work, and popularity of Robert Griffin III, a Washington Redskins quarterback who emerged as a professional football star as a rookie in 2012.

ISBN 978-1-60818-475-0
1. Griffin, Robert, III. 1990– —Juvenile literature. 2. Football players—United States—Biography—Juvenile literature. 3. Quarterbacks (Football)—United States—History—Juvenile literature. I. Title.
GV939.G775B64 2013
796.332092—dc23 [B]   2013014261

FIRST EDITION
9 8 7 6 5 4 3 2 1